HEINEMANN ELT GUIDED READERS

IN

MA

The Woman of Iron

HEINEMANN ELT

HEINEMANN ELT GUIDED READERS

INTERMEDIATE LEVEL

Series Editor: John Milne

The Heinemann ELT Guided Readers provide a choice of enjoyable reading material for learners of English. The series is published at five levels – Starter, Beginner, Elementary, Intermediate and Upper. At **Intermediate Level**, the control of content and language has the following main features:

Information Control
Information which is vital to the understanding of the story is presented in an easily assimilated manner and is repeated when necessary. Difficult allusion and metaphor are avoided and cultural backgrounds are made explicit.

Structure Control
Most of the structures used in the Readers will be familiar to students who have completed an elementary course of English. Other grammatical features may occur, but their use is made clear through context and re-inforcement. This ensures that the reading, as well as being enjoyable, provides a continual learning situation for the students. Sentences are limited in most cases to a maximum of three clauses and within sentences there is a balanced use of adverbial and adjectival phrases. Great care is taken with pronoun reference.

Vocabulary Control
There is a basic vocabulary of approximately 1,600 words. Help is given to the students in the form of illustrations, which are closely related to the text.

Glossary Словарь специфич. терминов
Some difficult words and phrases in this book are important for understanding the story. Some of these words are explained in the story, some are shown in the pictures, and others are marked with a number like this ... [3]. Words with a number are explained in the Glossary on page 91.

Contents

	A Note About This Story	*4*
	The People in This Story	*5*
1	'I Don't Want My Feet Bound!'	7
2	'Mei-Ying's Feet Will Be Bound!'	14
3	'We Cannot Go to America!'	21
4	'Our Lives Are Different Now'	28
5	'Earthquake!'	34
6	'*Ho sea fat choi!*'	39
7	'Why Can't We Use American Banks?'	45
8	'Chinese People Can't Go Inside the Bank'	51
9	The First United States–Chinese Bank	56
10	'Every Dollar in the Bank is Safe'	65
11	'Our Customers Want Their Money Back'	71
12	'$5 000 000 Are Missing'	78
	Points for Understanding	86
	Glossary	91
	List of Titles at Intermediate Level	95

A Note About This Story

This story is about the life of Mei-Ying Kan. She was born in China in 1898.

Her family was rich. Her grandfather owned a shoe shop in a rich part of Canton. Mei-Ying's father, Da-Wei, worked in the shoe shop with his father.

The story begins when Mei-Ying is a little girl. Her parents wanted Mei-Ying's feet to be bound[1]. People in China thought that women with very small feet were pretty. If a girl did not have her feet bound, it was difficult to find a husband for her. Women with bound feet could not walk easily. Servants carried them everywhere.

In 1898, there were many poor people in China and only a few rich people. The government was not strong. People thought that there would be a revolution. Rich people, like Mei-Ying's parents, were afraid that they would lose everything if they stayed in China.

Mei-Ying and her parents left China in 1904 before the first Chinese Revolution in 1911. They went to live in San Francisco, California. There, Mei-Ying's father and grandfather worked very hard and became rich. But Mei-Ying did not want to be a traditional Chinese woman. She wanted to work and to be independent.

The People in This Story

Kwok-Wah
Grandfather

Da-Wei
Father

Yim-Ping
Mother

Mr Bradford

Mei-Ying
('May') Daughter

1

'I Don't Want My Feet Bound!'

Canton, 1903

'No, I won't!'

'But Mei-Ying —'

'I don't want to!'

'But Mei-Ying! You don't want big ugly feet when you grow up, do you? Only servants have big feet!' Yim-Ping Kan smiled. She pointed to her own tiny feet and the beautiful little shoes that she was wearing.

'Look at my feet,' she said. 'Do you see how tiny they are? Don't you want beautiful little feet like mine when you grow up?'

Yim-Ping looked at her feet. She was proud of her tiny feet and she liked her pretty shoes. She had hundreds of pairs of shoes to wear. She was a rich woman. Her husband owned a large shoe shop in the best street in Canton. The shop was very successful and her husband made a lot of money. Yim-Ping had a beautiful house and lovely clothes to wear. The Kans ate meat every day. And now Yim-Ping's daughter, Mei-Ying, was going to have her feet bound. Mei-Ying was going to have beautiful, tiny feet like her mother. Mei-Ying was going to marry a rich man. She was going to have servants to do all her work. She was going to have children. Yim-Ping nodded her head and smiled. It was a good life for a woman.

The five-year-old child looked at her mother's tiny feet. She looked at the expensive furniture and the beautiful clothes in her mother's bedroom. She looked at the pretty combs[2] on her mother's dressing-table. She shook her head.

'No! No, Mother, I don't want to have feet like yours!' she shouted. 'Your feet are horrible! You can't run, you can't jump, you can't walk properly. You can't do anything! You have to be carried all the time. I don't want to be carried! I want to walk!'

'Mei-Ying, listen to me.' Yim-Ping looked at herself in the mirror on her dressing-table. She turned her head to one side. She liked her new hair-style.

'You're five years old now, Daughter,' she continued, 'and you must understand. You are very lucky. You come from a very good family. Your father is a rich man.'

Yim-Ping paused[3]. She began to put on her make-up, slowly and carefully. First she wiped her face with a cloth. Next she put smooth white powder all over her face and finally she put a little red powder on her cheeks. Then she started speaking to her daughter again.

'Your father will find you a good husband, a rich husband. You will live in a big house. You won't have to work. You will be an important lady. You will have servants to look after you,' Yim-Ping said.

'But I don't want to be a lady!' Mei-Ying shouted. 'I don't want a husband and a big house and servants! I want to work. I want to have a job! I don't want my feet bound! I've seen your feet! They're horrible! And you've only got your big toes. What happened to all your other toes? Did somebody cut them off?'

Yim-Ping spoke angrily.

'No, Mother, I don't want to have feet like yours!'

'Don't be silly, Mei-Ying! Of course not! Nobody cut my toes off. They – they got smaller and smaller. After a few years they disappeared. A woman from a good family doesn't need her toes! My feet are much prettier without my toes!'

'No, they aren't! Your feet are horrible! They smell bad!' Mei-Ying shouted. She turned and ran out of the room.

'Mei-Ying Kan! Where are you going? Come back here at once!'

But the child had already run out of the house and across the courtyard[4] in front of the house. She ran through the gate and into the narrow streets of the city.

Yim-Ping shouted and a young servant-girl ran into the room.

'Ah-Mei! Mei-Ying has run out of the house! Go after her and bring her back! Go quickly!'

The servant-girl turned and ran out of the door.

Out in the streets of Canton, Mei-Ying ran towards the river. The servant-girl, Ah-Mei, sometimes took Mei-Ying this way, but Mei-Ying had never been out of the house alone. Her mother said that the streets of Canton were dangerous but Mei-Ying did not believe her.

'How can Mother know anything about the streets?' Mei-Ying thought.

It was true. Yim-Ping did not go out of the house very often. When she did go out, she was carried in a sedan.

Mei-Ying had played in the sedan. It was like a box with open sides and there was a seat inside the box. There were silk[5] curtains round the sides of the box. If you closed the curtains, nobody could see you – and you could not see anything or anybody. When her mother wanted to visit friends in other parts of the city, she got into the sedan in the courtyard of the house. Ah-Mei closed the curtains all round her. Then two servants picked up the sedan and carried it through the streets. Mei-Ying did not like to be carried in a box with the curtains closed. She liked to look at the people in the streets, at the shops and the temples[6], and she liked to watch the boats on the river.

Today there were some large boats on the river, too. Ah-Mei had told Mei-Ying that these boats sometimes went across the sea to other countries far away from China.

Suddenly, Mei-Ying heard a loud noise from one of the boats. There was a cockerel on the boat.

'*Cock-a-doodle-doo!*' it cried. The cockerel had beautiful green feathers and a golden tail. The bird was tied to the boat by a string around its leg. Mei-Ying went closer to the boat. She watched as two sailors untied the cockerel. One man picked it up. The cockerel crowed loudly and tried to fly away. Some of its beautiful feathers fell onto the boat. The sailor held the cockerel so that it could not move. Then the other sailor pulled out a knife and cut off the cockerel's head.

'Look!' a little girl's voice said. 'My father is killing a cockerel for the goddess Machu.'

Mei-Ying turned and looked at the little girl standing beside her. She was about the same age as Mei-Ying. The girl's hair was short and her clothes were dirty.

'Machu?' Mei-Ying asked. 'Who's Machu?'

'Machu is a goddess. She protects sailors,' replied the little girl. 'Machu looks after our boats. She gives sailors safe journeys. We kill a cockerel and we pray to the goddess, Machu, before we start a long journey. Then we have good weather,' said the little girl.

Mei-Ying turned towards the little girl again.

'Are your parents going to bind your feet?' she asked.

The little girl looked at the flowers in Mei-Ying's hair. She looked at the silk clothes that Mei-Ying was wearing.

'Bind my feet?' The boat girl laughed. She lifted her dirty hand and touched the flowers in Mei-Ying's hair.

'Bind my feet? Of course not!' she said.

'Bind my feet? Of course not!' she said.

2

'Mei-Ying's Feet Will Be Bound!'

Canton, 1903

Mei-Ying turned and ran away from the little girl by the river. She ran into one of the narrow, crowded streets of the city. On one side, there were some wide stone steps. The steps led up to a temple. There was a wooden dragon[7] over the temple door. A crowd of beggars were sitting on the steps – men, women and thin, dirty childen. When someone entered the temple, the beggars held out their hands and asked for money.

Then a beggar woman saw Mei-Ying. The woman held out her hand. She looked ill. She was holding a baby. The baby was crying.

'Please! I need money for the baby! My baby is sick! Give me some money!'

Mei-Ying shook her head.

'I'm sorry! I haven't got any money!' she said.

Mei-Ying ran away from the beggar woman with the sick baby. She ran down another narrow street. People in the streets looked at her. Mei-Ying was alone. Young girls from rich families did not go into the streets alone, without their servants. Then Mei-Ying stopped. There was a man in front of one of the shops. There was a chain round his neck. Around his neck there was also a large wooden collar[8]. The collar was so large that the man could not reach his mouth or face with his hands. The man's face was very thin.

'I haven't got any money!'

Mei-Ying looked at the man. She ran into the shop.

'Why has that man got a piece of wood round his neck?' she asked the shopkeeper.

'He has the collar on because he's a thief!' the shopkeeper replied. 'He's a thief – he stole money from my shop! And that,' said the shopkeeper, pointing to the man, 'is what happens to thieves.'

'But he can't eat – he can't drink ...'

The shopkeeper said nothing. He turned and went back into his shop.

Mei-Ying walked slowly out of the shop.

'Water, water,' the thief whispered[9]. His mouth was so dry that he could only whisper to the people who passed by him. Two small boys came up to him. They were carrying a bucket of dirty water.

'Water? You want water?' they shouted.

The boys threw the water over the man and they laughed as he tried to catch some water in his mouth.

'Thief! Dirty thief!' they shouted.

Mei-Ying began to run. She wanted to find Hsiang Lan Street. Hsiang Lan Street was one of the most beautiful streets in Canton. It was a street where only rich people went to shop. Her father's shop was in this street.

Mei-Ying's grandfather, Kwok-Wah, had bought the shop many years before. He still worked in the shop with Mei-Ying's father, Da-Wei. Mei-Ying loved the shop. She loved the little shrine[10] at the back of the shop. Mei-Ying's father lit incense[11] in the shrine every morning when he opened the shop. He put the incense into the shrine and

'Water, water,' the thief whispered.

prayed for good business. Mei-Ying loved the sweet smell of the burning incense.

Mei-Ying soon found Hsiang Lan Street. She saw her father's shop and she ran towards it.

'Father? Are you here?' Mei-Ying cried out.

Mei-Ying's grandfather came out of the small room at the back of the shop.

'Mei-Ying! What are you doing here?' Kwok-Wah asked, surprised.

'Good morning, Grandfather. I'm looking for my father. Is he here?'

'But where's your servant? Why are you on your own?' asked Kwok-Wah.

Mei-Ying looked down at the floor of the shop and did not reply. Her grandfather turned to the back of the shop.

'Da-Wei! Come at once!' he shouted.

Mei-Ying's father came from the back room. He was about thirty years old. He was tall and strong, with a good-looking, clever face. He smiled when he saw Mei-Ying. He bent down and lifted her up gently in his arms.

'Hello, Little Flower[12]. What's the matter? What has happened? What are you doing here?' he asked softly.

'Father, I ran away from the house. I don't want my feet bound,' Mei-Ying whispered. 'I don't want to be like my mother.'

Kwok-Wah looked at his granddaughter.

'What is this? What are you saying?' Mei-Ying's grandfather said angrily. 'You don't want your feet bound? You don't want to be like your mother? This is nonsense! You are a very bad girl! When you grow up, we must find you a good husband – a husband with money. He must be a man from a good family. All women from good families have bound feet. If you have big feet, we will not be able to find a good husband for you. You will have to marry a servant and you will bring shame on your family!'

He stopped for a moment, then he turned to Da-Wei.

'Son,' Kwok-Wah said. 'You are too gentle with this child.'

Before Da-Wei could answer, the old man went into the back room of the shop.

'Wait here, Mei-Ying. I will talk to Grandfather.'

Mei-Ying's father put her down on the ground and followed the old man into the back room. It was a tiny room. There was just enough space for a table and two chairs. Mei-Ying's father sat down beside the old man.

'Father,' Da-Wei said. 'It's 1903. Things are changing in China now. You know that. The government is weak. They have no money. They have no power. The Chinese people do not want this government.' He spoke softly. 'Most people want a change – a revolution – a different way of life. There are too many poor people in China. There are too many beggars and too many sick people. You have heard the revolutionaries talking in the streets. Many people are talking about changing the way that we live. They are talking about changing the government. I think that things are going to change soon. And when things change, we may not be able to live in the old way. We may not be able to have servants and big houses. Maybe women from good families will have to work.'

The old man laughed.

'How can there be good families with no servants?' he said. 'How can women from good families work? These things will never happen! It's impossible!'

'Everything is possible, Father,' Da-Wei answered. 'Many people say that soon no woman will have her feet bound – not even women from the best families.'

The old man stood up. 'This is nonsense! Things will never change in China! And decisions for this family will not be made by a child! Mei-Ying's feet will be bound!'

3

'We Cannot Go to America!'

Canton, 1904

'You want to go to America?' Yim-Ping looked at her husband unhappily. 'But *gweilo* – foreigners – live in America! We cannot go to America!'

It was after dinner. The servants had put chairs and a table outside the Kan house in the garden. The family was enjoying the cool evening air. Mei-Ying was staring into the garden.

'There are a lot of *gweilo* in Canton, too, you know,' Da-Wei said. 'They have been living here and they have been doing business for many years.'

'Well, I've heard some terrible stories about the *gweilo*. I've heard that they steal children and eat them!' replied Yim-Ping.

Da-Wei shook his head and laughed.

'No, that's nonsense!' he said. 'Those are stories told by the revolutionaries. The revolutionaries want to destroy the government. The government needs the foreigners' money. And the foreigners know a lot about business. If the foreigners leave China, the government will lose power.'

Da-Wei looked out across the garden. Then he turned towards Yim-Ping.

'Wife, there is going to be a revolution,' he said. 'I am sure of this. And I am sure that the revolution is going to happen soon. And when the revolution happens, we will

'You want to go to America?'

lose everything. We must leave China before it is too late. We must leave China before we lose everything.'

Kwok-Wah stood up.

'We cannot go to America!' the old man said angrily. 'Who will look after the family shrine? Who will burn incense at the shrine? Who will pray to the family gods?'

'But Father,' replied Da-Wei, 'we are a big family. You have other sons who will stay here in Canton. They can look after the family shrine and burn incense. Listen. There will be many members of the family[13] still living here in Canton. But after the revolution, they may need help. We will be able to help them. We will be able to send them money from America!'

'And what about my carved coffin[14]?' Kwok-Wah asked. 'That coffin cost me a lot of money. I saved money for my funeral, too. A man from a good family must have a big funeral and a beautiful coffin. What will happen to me in America?' he asked. 'What about my coffin?'

'Father,' replied Da-Wei gently, 'I do not think that we can take your coffin with us. It is too big.'

'I cannot go to America without my coffin. I cannot leave my coffin here. No more of this nonsense. We will stay in Canton.'

'Father,' said Da-Wei. 'I will buy you another coffin when we get to America. It will be even better than the one you have now.'

The old man went into the house and took a large book down from a shelf. He came back outside, carrying the book and a small wooden box. He put the heavy book down on the table, sat down on his chair and took the lid off the wooden box.

'We will ask the *I Ching*[15]. The *I Ching* is never wrong,' Kwok Wah said. 'My father and my father's father always used this book to help them make important decisions. The *I Ching* will tell us if we should go to America.'

He took some coins out of the box, shook them in one hand and threw them onto the table. He looked at the coins carefully. He picked up the coins and threw them five more times. Then he turned to the pages of the book. He read. Then he said:

'You must be very careful if you want good luck.
Sailing across the great sea does not bring good luck.'

Kwok-Wah shut the book.

'You heard the words of the *I Ching*,' he said. 'We must not go to America. We must stay in Canton.'

'Grandfather is right, Husband,' said Yim-Ping.

Da-Wei stood up.

'Listen,' he said, 'the *I Ching* was written more than five thousand years ago. How can we know that the answers in the *I Ching* are right? We must make our own decisions about our lives. Soon it will not be safe to live or to do business in Canton. If we stay here we will lose everything. Wife, you will not have any beautiful silk clothes or your servants. Father, you will not have your shop and you will not even have your coffin. The revolution will take all those things away. Canton will not be a safe place for our child. No. We must go to America.'

'But where will we live?' asked Yim-Ping. 'What will we eat? Where will we get our clothes?'

'We will live in San Francisco,' replied Da-Wei. 'There

'We will ask the I Ching.'

are many Chinese people living there. My cousin lives there. I wrote a letter to him. I received his reply this morning. He says that business is good in America. He says that Chinatown[16] in San Francisco is like Canton. He says that we will be safe there.'

Da-Wei stopped talking. Mei-Ying was still staring into the garden.

'And what about you, Mei-Ying?' Da-Wei went on. 'Do you want the family to go to America?'

Mei-Ying got up slowly and smiled at her father.

'I shall like it very much, Father. I am very happy that we are going to San Francisco.' Then she stood up and went into the house.

Yim-Ping shook her head.

'She is a strange child!' she said.

Walking was painful for Mei-Ying. Her feet had been bound for several months now. The pain did not stop in the night or in the day. She went up the stairs and opened her bedroom door. She got onto her bed with difficulty[17]. She put her hand under the thick, heavy mattress and pulled out a small piece of silk.

There was a poem written on the silk. It was Mei-Ying's favourite poem. It was written by Qin Jin.

Qin Jin was a Chinese woman from a good family and Qin Jin's feet had been bound. When she grew up, her father had chosen a husband for her. But Qin Jin did not love her husband. After a few years she left her husband. She left her two children. She became a revolutionary. She unbound her feet and left China. Qin Jin wrote the poem after she had unbound her feet and had left China.

Sun and moon have no light and the earth is dark;
It is difficult to be a woman. Who can help us?
I sold my jewellery to pay for this journey across the sea,
I am leaving my family and my country.
I unbind my feet and I am free from a thousand years of prison.
All women must be free.
I unbind my feet, I free myself. And I weep.

Mei-Ying read the poem and put the piece of silk back under the mattress. She sat for a moment and looked down at her feet. Her feet had been bound for less than a year.

'I unbind my feet and I am free from a thousand years of prison,' she whispered.

Mei-Ying took her shoes off slowly. She began to take off the long, tight strips of cloth that bound her feet.

'All women must be free.'

When Mei-Ying had finished unbinding the cloth, she stared at her feet. She moved her feet up and down. This hurt very much, but she continued to move her feet, up and down, then from side to side. Then slowly, very slowly, she walked to the window. She looked at the dark blue evening sky and breathed the warm air.

'America. America!' she whispered.

4

'Our Lives Are Different Now'

Chinatown, San Francisco, 1905

'Mei-Ying Kan! Answer me! I know that you're there! I know that you can hear me! Answer me!'

Yim-Ping went across the main room of the apartment to the closed door of her daughter's room. She knocked on the door, then listened for a moment.

'Mei-Ying! Mei-Ying! Open this door!' she shouted. Yim-Ping listened again. There was no sound from inside the room. She shook her head and knocked on the door again.

'Mei-Ying! What is all this nonsense? What am I going to do with you? First you want to wear ugly foreign clothes! Then you want to learn the *gweilos'* ugly language! And now you want to change your name! Your name is Mei-Ying! Why do you want another name?'

At last Mei-Ying replied. Her voice came from inside the bedroom.

'Because American people don't know how to write Mei-Ying!' she shouted. 'And they can't say it properly, either! We're living in America now, Mother! We have to live like Americans! We must wear American clothes and talk like Americans. We're not in Canton any more. We're in San Francisco! We've been here for almost a year! Our lives are different now and we have to change, too!'

Yim-Ping knocked on the bedroom door again.

'Well, I'm not going to call you a foreign name like a

gweilo! Your name is Mei-Ying!' she shouted.

Yim-Ping stopped and listened. Then she knocked harder on the door.

'Mei-Ying, go to your father's shop and ask him for some money,' Yim-Ping shouted. 'Our cousin is coming to eat with us this evening and there's no rice in the house. Mei-Ying! Go now!'

There was no answer. 'What a strange child,' she thought.

Yim-Ping could hear the noise of the busy street outside the house. She went to sit on one of the chairs beside the table in the middle of the room. She waited there for a few minutes. There was still no answer from Mei-Ying's room. At last, Yim-Ping got up and went into the dark, tiny kitchen. She looked in the cupboards and on the shelves.

'What shall we do? There's no rice! Oh, that child!' Yim-Ping shut the cupboard door loudly and went back to Mei-Ying's room.

'All right! All right!' she shouted angrily. 'I'll call you that horrible *gweilo* name if I have to – May, May, go to your father. Ask him for some money and then buy rice, chicken and pork for tonight. And buy some vegetables, too, May. There. I've said it – May. You can come out now!'

The bedroom door opened and Mei-Ying came out. She was smiling.

Yim-Ping did not smile. 'What a terrible child,' she thought.

'Now go quickly,' Yim-Ping said to Mei-Ying.

'Certainly, Mother,' May replied. 'Thank you for calling

me by my new name. From today, I am going to live like an American girl. I shall learn English and wear American clothes. I am starting a new life!'

May went out into the narrow streets of Chinatown. It was a beautiful spring day and the streets were crowded with both American and Chinese people.

She hurried past restaurants lit by brightly-coloured lanterns and small shops selling Chinese food. As she turned a corner into Powell Street, Mei-Ying began to walk more slowly. She loved Powell Street.

'This is where Chinatown ends and America begins!' she said to herself.

She read the street signs. She said the names slowly to herself, 'The United States Bank. California Street.'

Then she turned round and stopped. Chinatown was behind her. She looked across at the hill rising up from the other side of the highway. She said the words slowly, 'Nob Hill'.

The words were strange. She stared at the huge houses on the hill. This was where San Francisco's most successful businessmen lived. They had big houses behind high gates. There were beautiful gardens around the houses. She watched the big, shiny cars drive off the highway and drive up the hill. The drivers in the cars wore caps and uniforms. The men who sat in the backs of the cars wore suits, hats and overcoats. May looked especially at the women in the cars.

'What lovely hair and clothes!' she thought. 'They are all so beautiful.'

After a few minutes, May turned and went back into

'This is where Chinatown ends and America begins!

the narrow, crowded streets of Chinatown. She walked to her father's shoe shop. The shop was successful. Her father and grandfather worked very hard, and now the business was making a lot of money[18]. Her mother could buy new clothes and there was plenty of money for food. And there was enough extra money every month to send to their relatives in Canton. May waited for some customers to leave and then she greeted her father. He smiled when he saw her.

'May! Hello! Is everything all right?' he asked.

May nodded. 'Your cousin is coming to eat with us tonight. Mother wants me to buy some food for the meal,' she replied.

Da-Wei led May into a small room at the back of the shop. It was a storeroom. There were shelves all round the room. And on the shelves there were hundreds of shoe boxes. Da-Wei took down one of the boxes and opened it. The box was full of money. He took out some banknotes and gave them to May.

'Father?'

'What is it?'

May watched as her father put the rest of the notes back into the box and put the box back on the shelf.

'Why do you keep your money in shoe boxes?' she asked.

Da-Wei was surprised.

'Why do you ask?' he said. 'Everybody keeps their money in shoe boxes.'

'Not Americans,' she replied. 'In America, people put their money in banks.'

'Ah! But not Chinese people, Little Flower,' Da-Wei said to her. 'Chinese people can't use banks. We can't use banks and we can't live outside Chinatown.'

'Can't use banks? Can't live outside Chinatown? But why can't we?' May asked.

Her father laughed again, but his voice was angry.

'You ask too many questions, May. Now go and get that food for your mother. I'll see you tonight.'

5

'Earthquake!'

San Francisco, 1906

May opened her eyes. There was no sound from the street outside and inside the apartment it was quiet. Her grandfather and her mother and father were still asleep. She picked up the book from the table beside her bed and got up quietly. She went over to the window and sat down beside it.

The street outside was still dark. Most of the shops were shut but one or two restaurants had opened their doors. May saw the boy who worked in the kitchen of the restaurant opposite their apartment. He looked up at her window and waved his hand. He saw her there every day, reading her books.

May waved back at the kitchen boy. She pulled a warm blanket round her shoulders and opened the book. The light from the restaurant fell on the book. She began to read the title slowly, '*The Adventures of Huckleberry Finn*, by Mark Twain.'

She did not understand many of the words in the book, but the pictures helped her to understand the story. Whenever she read a word she did not understand, she looked it up in the dictionary and said the word softly, again and again. May loved getting up in early morning, before the noise of the day began. She was learning English fast. Soon she would understand everything!

Suddenly, a glass of water on the table beside the bed

shook slightly. May was reading. She was enjoying the story. She went on reading. Then the window began to shake. May looked up from her book.

'What's happening?' she thought.

Now the water in the glass was shaking so much that some water spilt onto the table. May tried to pick up the glass before it fell, but she was too late. The glass fell over and the water spilt onto the table.

Then the kitchen boy ran out of the restaurant. He stopped in the middle of the street. He was scared.

'Earthquake! Earthquake! Wake up everyone!' he shouted. 'Get out!'

May threw down her book. She tried to stand up but the floor started to move under her feet and she fell down. May tried to stand up again. She put one hand against the wall and she tried to hold the chair with the other hand. She was really scared now. But she couldn't stand up. The glass on May's table fell onto the floor and broke. Then she heard the crash[19] of plates and bowls breaking as they hit the floor in the kitchen, and the crash of cooking pots as they fell off the shelves. She heard the screams of frightened people outside. She heard her mother screaming and her father shouting.

'May! Earthquake!' shouted Da-Wei. 'Quick! Help your mother! We've got to get out of the apartment!'

Yim-Ping could not walk because of her bound feet. She fell over and could not get up. Da-Wei and Kwok-Wah were trying to carry her out of the building. May went to help her father and together they carried Yim-Ping down the stairs and into the street outside.

Many people were running out of their houses and into the street. Most people were still in their night-clothes. Some were holding bundles of clothes, some were carrying their family shrine, others were carrying their children. There was the noise of crying babies and children, shouting men and screaming women and the terrible noise of houses falling.

Many, many buildings fell down. May and her family stood and watched their apartment. Would it also fall down? Then, suddenly, the earthquake stopped. There was silence for a moment. Nobody moved.

'Don't go back inside the buildings,' someone shouted, 'they might fall down and kill you!'

'Grandfather, you stay with Yim-Ping,' Da-Wei shouted. 'May, come with me!'

'But Father! Where are we going? We can't leave Grandfather and Mother. There might be another earthquake!' May shouted, as she ran after her father.

'The shop! We have to get to the shop!' he shouted back at her. 'There might be a fire!'

There were bricks and big pieces of wood in the streets and there were crowds of people. They all looked scared.

Da-Wei and May saw a small fire in one of the buildings. Da-Wei ran faster.

'Look! Fire!' he shouted. 'Run quickly, May!'

Many of the shop windows that they passed were broken. Some people were stealing anything that they could find. Da-Wei and May passed another burning building, then another. The little fires began to spread quickly

Many people were running out of their houses and into the street.

through the wooden buildings.

May knew why her father wanted to get to their shop quickly. There were shoe boxes full of money – paper money – on the shelves of the storeroom. All the money they had would burn in a few minutes. They had to get to the shop before a fire started. Or before someone stole their money.

Fires were spreading quickly from house to house. Soon, many of the buildings in the city were burning. The fires burnt for all that day and all the next night. They went on burning for three whole days. Thousands of families watched as their homes or businesses were destroyed.

Five hundred people died in the earthquake. Most of San Francisco's city centre and Chinatown were burnt down. And May's home and her father's shoe shop were among the thousands of buildings and businesses that were destroyed in the fire.

In the terrible days after the earthquake, thousands of people had to go to Oakland. Oakland was not far from San Francisco by boat.

The Kan family stood quietly on the boat as it left the harbour. San Francisco was still burning. As the boat moved out into the bay, the Kans looked away from the fire and towards Oakland. They had nothing with them but the clothes that they were wearing – and a few shoe boxes.

6

'Ho sea fat choi!'

Oakland, 1916

It was the first day of the Chinese New Year[20]. May was eighteen years old. She was tall and pretty. She had long shiny black hair. She wore American clothes. She loved American things – jazz, baseball, apple pie[21] – but she loved all the traditional Chinese celebrations[22] as well. She especially enjoyed the Chinese New Year. On this day each year, she wrote Chinese characters[23] on pieces of red paper. Then she stuck the red paper on the walls of the apartment.

'These words will bring good luck during the New Year,' she thought.

The day before, she helped her mother sweep the apartment. Also on that day, all the family bathed and everyone wore new clothes.

Nobody swept the house on Chinese New Year's Day. Nobody wanted to sweep all the luck out of the house. And nobody took a bath – it was important not to wash good luck away. May's grandfather and her father gave her little red packets with money inside, and her father burnt incense at the family shrine.

Now the family was sitting round a table in the living-room. It was time for the special New Year's Day meal. Chinese families do not eat meat on New Year's Day, but Yim-Ping had made a wonderful meal. There were bowls of soup, rice and vegetable dishes, and delicious little cakes and sweets.

The men drank rice wine, and the women drank tiny cups of tea. Yim-Ping gave Da-Wei a bowl of oysters and seaweed[24]. The Chinese words for 'oyster' – *ho sea* – and 'seaweed' – *fat choi* – sound like the Chinese words for 'good business' and 'prosperity'[25].

'*Ho sea fat choi*, Grandfather!' said Yim-Ping. '*Ho sea fat choi*, Husband!'

Da-Wei smiled without speaking. He looked tired.

'*Ho sea* – good business,' Yim-Ping said again and gave Da-Wei some more oysters and seaweed. 'Now we shall have plenty of good business in the New Year,' she said. '*Ho sea fat choi* – Good business and prosperity,' she added, putting more oysters and seaweed into Grandfather's bowl.

May looked at her father and grandfather. Da-Wei did not look well. And her grandfather was looking very old.

'Father?'

'Yes, May?'

'Father, eleven years ago, when we arrived in America, you and Grandfather worked very hard to start the shoe shop business in San Francisco,' May said. 'Then, less than two years after we arrived, there was the earthquake in 1906. Our house and the shop in San Francisco burnt down. We had to come to Oakland. You had to start the business again.

'You and Grandfather worked very hard on your new business here in Oakland. You still sent money back to the relatives in Canton, every month. Business is good again now. But you're not well, Father. You and Grandfather are tired. You're working too hard. There is too much

'Ho sea fat choi, Husband!'

work for you to do.'

Da-Wei put down his chopsticks[26] and looked at his daughter. He drank some wine.

'And who will do the work if we don't, Little Flower?' he asked.

'Me,' said May. 'I can help you. I'm not a child now, Father. I'm eighteen years old. I want to work in the shop. Please let me.'

'What?' May's grandfather said. 'My granddaughter work in a shop? What are you thinking of? You're a woman! You come from a good family! You can't work in a shop!'

May filled her grandfather's cup with wine.

'But Grandfather, please listen,' May replied. 'I speak English very well and I know how American people do business[27]. It is different from our way of doing business. I can help you. We could begin to do business with the Americans. We could sell shoes to them. We would have more customers and we would do very good business.'

May picked up some *ho sea* with her chopsticks. She put them into her grandfather's bowl. Grandfather looked at the oysters. He picked one up and put it in his mouth.

'Well ... ' He ate the oyster slowly. 'I don't understand the *gweilo*'s language. And you, Son, you don't always understand what they are saying. And neither of us can speak their language. That is not good. But you can speak English, May.'

Yim-Ping put down her tea cup and looked at the old man.

'Grandfather! What are you saying? It is not possible!'

she said. 'The child must stay at home. Young girls from our family do not work in shops. She will never find a good husband if she goes to work in a shop. No man will want to marry a shop girl! No, she must stay at home and help me in the house. That is the place for a woman of good family.'

May touched her mother's arm.

'But Mother,' she said, 'Father and Grandfather are tired. They have been working too hard. I am afraid that they will become ill, and what will happen to the shop then? And Mother,' she added, 'if I were at the shop, father could get you a servant to help you with the shopping and with the work in the house.'

There was a silence.

'Well,' Da-Wei looked at his father. 'What do you think, Father?'

Kwok-Wah put down his bowl and chopsticks on the table. 'May!' he said. 'Bring me the *I Ching*. Then we will know what to do.'

May took the bowls and dishes off the table. She took the heavy book and the box of coins off a shelf and gave them to her grandfather. She sat quietly as her grandfather threw the coins. He looked at the coins and opened the book. He turned the pages slowly.

'These are the words of the *I Ching*,' Grandfather said.

'She should not do what she wants.

She must prepare the food in the home.

If you wait, you will be lucky.'

Nobody said anything. There was a long silence. Yim-Ping was the first to speak.

'Well, Grandfather,' she said. 'This is America. People live differently here. We must make decisions for ourselves. In China, a woman should stay at home and look after the house. That is true. But in America, many women work outside their homes.' She looked at her daughter. 'Perhaps May is right. She's a clever girl. You would not be so tired if she helped you in the shop. Perhaps I can cook and clean the house without her.'

Da-Wei looked at his father. Kwok-Wah nodded his head. Da-Wei turned towards May.

'Very well, child. You can work in the shop,' he said. 'We will see what happens.' He held out his cup and Yim-Ping filled it with wine. 'You can start work in the shop after the New Year holiday.'

7

'Why Can't We Use American Banks?'

Oakland, 1919

For the next three years, May worked hard in the shop. She had new ideas. She was young and she liked to wear American clothes and shoes. She bought American fashion magazines. She saw that Americans liked new fashions – new colours and new styles of clothes and shoes.

'We'll sell shoes in the new styles and fashions in our shop,' she thought.

Soon Americans began to buy shoes from Da-Wei's shoe shop. Americans often bought new shoes because there was a new fashion every summer and every winter.

Then May changed the inside of the shop. She put a large Chinese carpet on the floor. She brought comfortable chairs for the customers to sit on. She put large mirrors on the walls. A young American woman came to work in the shop.

May worked many hours every day but she enjoyed her work very much. She was the first person to arrive at the shop in the mornings. She turned on the lights and opened the doors. And she was always the last person to leave in the evenings.

More and more Americans came to the shop. They spent a lot of money on shoes.

'Americans like sports,' she thought one day as she looked at a fashion magazine. 'Perhaps we can sell sports shoes, too. Perhaps we can also sell bags and suitcases.'

May always had new ideas. Her father smiled when she spoke to him about her ideas. And he always said 'yes' when she wanted to try a new idea in the shop.

The Kan family made more and more money. Da-Wei continued to send money back to the relatives in Canton, but there was always a good profit[28] at the end of every month.

'Father,' May said one day. 'We'll soon have enough money to open another shop!'

Da-Wei did not answer. He counted the money carefully and put it into shoe boxes. He put the boxes on the shelves in the storeroom.

One evening, Da-Wei was counting the money as usual.

'Father?' May said.

'What is it, Little Flower?' he said.

'Father, I've been thinking about our money. It's not safe to keep all this money in shoe boxes. Someone might steal it. We could lose it all in a fire.'

'Yes, I know, May, I know,' Da-Wei replied. 'But what can we do with it? Do you want me to put it under my mattress? We can't put the money in a bank. You know that Chinese people aren't allowed to use the banks in America. We can't use banks and we aren't allowed to live outside Chinatown!'

Da-Wei smiled at his daughter.

'Don't worry, May,' he said. 'The money is safe in those boxes.'

'But Father,' May said, 'you've got thousands of dollars

'It's not safe to keep all this money in shoe boxes.'

here! What will happen if somebody steals all this money? What will happen if there's another earthquake or fire? We might lose everything again.'

Da-Wei said nothing.

'What would mother say if we lost all our money?' May asked. 'And what about our relatives in Canton? What will they do if we don't send them any money? I think that we should go to a bank. We live in America – we use American money – why can't we use American banks?'

'Well, May,' said Da-Wei, 'we can go to a bank. But I'm sure that they won't be interested in doing business with Chinese people!'

May stood up and took down some shoe boxes from the shelves.

'Thank you, Father,' she said. 'Why don't we go to a bank tomorrow?'

The next day, Da-Wei and May stood outside the main branch[29] of the United States Bank. It was a large stone building on a wide street in the centre of Oakland. There were steps going up to the large wooden doors of the bank. Two guards were standing outside the bank. They wore grey uniforms and they carried guns. The men and women who went in and out of the bank wore expensive American clothes, good shoes and fashionable hats. Da-Wei looked down at his Chinese clothes. He stopped outside the bank and he looked up at the big stone building.

'May! I can't go in there!' he whispered. 'Look at my clothes! Nobody in the bank will speak to me! Let's go back to the shop!'

But May was already at the top of the steps. Da-Wei watched as she went up to one of the guards and spoke to him. The guard listened to her, then he went into the bank. May looked down at her father and waved her hand.

'Someone from the bank is coming to see us!' she shouted.

Da-Wei and May did not have to wait for very long. The guard came out of the bank with a tall man.

'Good day,' the man said to May. 'How may I help you?'

May shook hands with the man. She talked to him for a few minutes. Then they both walked down the steps to where Da-Wei was waiting with his shoe boxes.

'Father, this is Mr Bradford,' said May. 'He works in the bank. I told him that you have some money to put in his bank.'

Da-Wei gave one of the shoe boxes to the banker. The American opened it and looked quickly at the bank notes.

'Do all those boxes have money in them?' the banker asked.

'Yes, Mr Bradford,' May replied. 'My father would like to put all this money into your bank.'

'I see.' The American looked at the boxes again.

'There are thousands of dollars in these boxes,' he said.

'Yes,' May replied. 'Thousands of dollars.'

The big American looked at May carefully. He looked down the street and then back at the bank. He did not look very happy.

'Well ... er, lady, we don't have Chinese customers at our bank,' he said.

'There is a lot of money here, Mr Bradford,' Da-Wei

said slowly. 'And there is no difference between American dollars if I own the money or if you own the money. I am Chinese, but my money is American.'

Mr Bradford thought for a moment. 'Well, yes, yes, it is,' he said slowly. He smiled a little and then nodded his head. 'Well, perhaps we can help you, Mr ... ?'

May smiled.

'Our name is Kan, Mr Bradford,' she said. 'I think you are doing the right thing. And Mr Bradford — ?'

'Yes, Miss Kan?'

'There are many Chinese businessmen like my father,' she said. 'They might also be interested in putting their money in your bank. Some of them are much richer than my father. Unfortunately, many of them do not speak English very well. Some Chinese businessmen do not understand the American way of banking[30]. I know how Chinese people do business and I also understand how Americans do business. Perhaps I can help you.'

The tall American looked down at the young woman. She looked at him calmly.

'Would you like to think about my idea, Mr Bradford?' she asked. 'I can give you two days to decide.'

8

'Chinese People Can't Go Inside the Bank'

Oakland, 1919

It was the first day of May's new job at the bank. She got up very early that morning. She had not slept much during the night. She was too excited.

May put on a new dress, jacket and new shoes, and brushed her long hair until it shone. She was nervous and did not eat any breakfast. She drank a cup of tea, said goodbye to her mother and father, and stepped out into the early morning sunshine.

It was a beautiful sunny day. May felt excited as she walked through the busy streets towards the bank. This was the first day of a new life for her!

Mr Bradford was waiting outside the bank for her. But he did not take her into the building through the big wooden doors at the top of the steps. Instead, he took her to the back of the bank building. There was a small door onto the street there. They went in through this door. Behind the door there was a narrow, dark corridor. Mr Bradford took May along the corridor into a small room. There was no carpet on the floor.

The only furniture in the room was a wooden table and a hard wooden chair. Although it was a lovely sunny day outside, no sunlight came through the small window high up in one of the walls. Mr Bradford turned on a lamp on the desk. A weak light filled the room.

Mr Bradford was embarrassed.

'I hope that we can find you a better room soon,' he said.

'I can work here,' May said. 'But Mr Bradford, where can I meet customers? Where can I meet people who want to do business in the bank?'

'Well, Miss Kan,' he said. 'You must see them outside the bank.'

'Outside the bank? What do you mean? Where outside? On the steps?'

Mr Bradford became more embarrassed. His face was red.

'No, no,' he said.

'Well, where?' asked May.

'There's a small street behind the bank,' he replied. 'There's a door to the street down this corridor. You can meet customers in the street. Then you can do your paperwork[31] here, in this room.'

'So I can bring Chinese money into the bank,' May said. 'But I can't bring Chinese people into the building. And I can work in this room at the back of the bank. And if I stay in this room and do my work in the street nobody from the bank will see me. Is that right, Mr Bradford?'

'That is correct, Miss Kan,' the big American replied. 'I'm sorry, but it's not my decision. Now, I must get back to my work.'

Mr Bradford left quickly and shut the door behind him. May sat down at the table and looked round the dark, cold little room. She did not like the room. And she did

'I hope that we can find you a better room soon.'

not want to do business in the street behind the bank.

At supper that evening, Da-Wei, Kwok-Wah and Yim-Ping looked at May. They wanted to hear about her first day at work. But she said nothing. She did not feel hungry. Yim-Ping had cooked a special dinner because it was May's first day at the bank.

'What's the matter, child?' she asked. 'Why don't you eat? Why don't you say anything? Did you have a bad day? What happened?'

May looked unhappily at the dishes of food on the table.

'I'm sorry, Mother,' she said. 'I'm not hungry. It was horrible at the bank. I have to work in a dark little room at the back of the building. And I have to meet Chinese customers in the street. I have to work in a street behind the bank!'

She filled the little tea cups with green tea.

'I've seen women take little dogs into the bank. But Chinese people can't go inside the bank. We have to stay in the street! The American people think that dogs are more important than Chinese people! I don't want to work like that. I'm not going back to the bank tomorrow! I'm sorry, Father. I should have stayed with you and Grandfather at the shoe shop!'

Yim-Ping began to put hot food in the bowls. She passed them to Kwok-Wah and Da-Wei. Then she spoke to her daughter.

'Mei-Ying, you are being very foolish,' she said. 'Did you think that you would have the best room in the bank? Think about what you have done, child. Your father is the first Chinese man to have an account in an American bank. You are the first Chinese person to work in an American bank! And now you are unhappy because you have a small, dark room! You must wait for a few months before you decide to leave your job, my child.

'But,' Yim-Ping went on, 'I do not think that you will leave your job. It is new and strange now, but you will soon begin to enjoy your work.'

Da-Wei and May both stared at Yim-Ping. Yim-Ping had changed! She did not speak like an old-fashioned Chinese wife and mother any more!

There was a silence in the room. The food began to get cold.

'Think, daughter,' Yim-Ping continued. 'This is only the beginning. You are young, you are only twenty-one years old! You have so many ideas, there are so many things that you want to do.' She touched May's face gently with her hand.

'I believe that you will be successful in your life. I am happy for you. I have lived my life as a wife. But you can be different. You can live your life as you want to live it. You're starting work in that bank. It isn't easy. But you can do well, if you work hard. One day, you will have the best room in the bank!'

She put a bowl of food in front of May. 'Now eat your food before it is cold.'

9

The First United States–Chinese Bank

Oakland, 1936

Yim-Ping and Da-Wei were sitting together after supper one evening. Seventeen years had passed since May had begun to work in the United States Bank.

Yim-Ping and Da-Wei now lived in a beautiful big house near the centre of Oakland. A young Chinese girl helped Yim-Ping with the housework and cooking.

Da-Wei had five successful shoe shops. He did not have to work so hard now. He came home from work early in the evening.

This evening, Yim-Ping was looking at a large book. The book was full of newspaper articles. She passed the book to Da-Wei.

'Look, Husband,' she said. 'I have put all the newspaper articles about May into a book. Do you remember the first time that there was an article about May in a newspaper? Do you remember how happy and excited we were?'

'Yes, I remember,' Da-Wei replied. 'It was one of the articles about the first United States–Chinese Bank, wasn't it?'

'Yes,' said Yim-Ping. 'She became a director[32] of the first United States–Chinese Bank only six years after she began to work in the bank. She worked so hard! We were so proud[33] of her that day, weren't we, Husband?'

Yim-Ping pointed to the next newspaper article.

'Yes,' said Da-Wei. 'She was the first Chinese director

of the first Chinese bank in the United States – and she was only twenty-seven years old!'

April 1925

THE FIRST UNITED STATES–CHINESE BANK OPENS IN OAKLAND

THE first United States–Chinese Bank opened in Chinatown, Oakland, today. A large crowd of people watched the opening of the bank. The opening began with Chinese lion dances[34]. Chinese people believe that these traditional dances bring good luck.

Miss May Kan is the director of the new bank. She told newspaper reporters:

'Today is a lucky day for all the Chinese people living here in Oakland. From today, Chinese people have their own bank. At last, they can keep their money safely. And from today, Chinese people will be able to borrow[35] money from the bank to start their own businesses. We hope to lend[36] money to anyone who is starting a business and who needs our help. This bank is the first branch of a Chinese bank. We hope to open more branches of Chinese banks in Hong Kong and in China as well. This is the start of a great day for all Chinese businessmen and women, both in America and in the Far East!'

Yim-ping pointed to the next newspaper article.

April 1930

THE UNITED STATES–CHINESE BANK IS FIVE YEARS OLD

TODAY is the fifth anniversary of the United States–Chinese Bank. Five hundred people were at a party at the St Moritz Hotel to celebrate the bank's birthday. Miss May Kan is a director of the United States–Chinese Bank. She talked about her work at the bank and her hopes of the future:

'Chinese people work hard and they are good at business. But things used to be difficult for them. Many Chinese people arrived in America with no money. They needed money to start their own business. They needed to borrow money. But Chinese people could not go into American banks. Things are different now. Things are very much better for Chinese people. Any Chinese person can borrow money from the United States–Chinese Bank to start their own business.

'We hope that the United States–Chinese Bank will soon have branches all over America, and then perhaps we will open branches in China, Hong Kong, Singapore and Malaya. Wherever there are Chinese people who need a bank, we hope to be there!'

'Look, husband! Here's a picture of that big party at the St Moritz Hotel! The party that celebrated the United States–Chinese Bank's fifth anniversary! And look at May! Doesn't she look beautiful?'

Da-Wei nodded.

'Yes. May's worked hard. She's done well,' he said.

Then Yim-Ping pointed to a big photo of May and an article from a fashionable women's magazine.

June 1931

A DAY IN THE LIFE OF MISS MAY KAN, BANKER

by Susanne Bates

'You are a famous bank director,' I said to Miss May Kan, director of the United States–Chinese Bank. 'You are a woman and you are Chinese. Very few women have important positions in banks in America. You were also the first Chinese person – man or woman – to work in an American bank. And you became a director of an American bank. How did you do it?'

May Kan was dressed in a black-and-white Dior[37] suit. She was sitting in her large office on the top floor of the bank building.

'It was hard work,' she answered, 'But I knew what I wanted. You have to know what you want. And you must never give up. When I was a very young girl, I wanted to have a job. I didn't want to stay at home and wait for my husband to get back from work. I wanted to work myself!'

'Tell me about your work each day,' *I said.*

'Well, I get up at five o'clock every morning. First I drink some tea. Then I take a shower and get dressed. My car and my driver arrive at 6.30 a.m. I'm at my office by seven o'clock. There are usually lots of letters to read. Then I read the business reports in the newspapers. After reading the newspapers, I usually have some meetings. There's a lot of paperwork. I usually get home at about eight o'clock in the evening. I have supper with my mother and father – my mother is a wonderful cook – and then I read more papers and documents. I usually work until one or two in the morning – I don't need much sleep. Then I go to bed for a few hours' rest. And I get up again at five in the morning.'

'Miss Kan, you were born in China, but you have lived most of your life in America. Are you Chinese or American?'

'That's a very difficult question. You see, I come from a traditional Chinese family. I was born in China before the Revolution. My mother came from a very good family. Before the Revolution, women from good families had bound feet. Women from good families stayed at home. They did not have to work. They had servants. But then our family came to America. Life was very different for women here in America! American women worked, they played sports, they dressed in comfortable clothes. They wore their hair in simple styles. I wanted to be just like an American girl! But as I grew older, I began to be interested in China again. We have many wonderful writers, poets and artists. So you see, I'm both Chinese and American.'

'Miss Kan, you say that your mother's feet were bound. Were your feet bound, too?'

'Yes. My feet were bound when I was five. But shortly afterwards, my father decided to come to America. I unbound my feet. My mother was very angry and told me that if I had big feet I would never get a husband. But I didn't want a husband. I wanted a job!'

'I remember the day that she first wore American clothes,' said Yim-Ping. 'It was soon after we arrived in San Francisco. I thought that she looked terrible. I did not like her wearing American clothes. But now I think that she looks beautiful in foreign clothes. I even like her big feet!' she said with a laugh.

Yim-Ping picked up the newspaper from the table and passed it to Da-Wei.

'Look,' she said, 'there's another article about May in the newspaper today. May is going to open branches of the United States–Chinese Bank in Hong Kong and China. Won't the relatives in Canton be surprised when they hear about this?'

BRANCHES OF UNITED STATES–CHINESE BANK OPEN IN HONG KONG AND CHINA

MISS MAY KAN, director of the United States–Chinese Bank, Oakland, travelled to the Far East today. She will be opening branches of the United States–Chinese Bank in Hong Kong, Canton and Shanghai. She will be in the Far East for two weeks. 'People need banks in the Far East,' Miss Kan said. 'We hope to open more branches in China in the future.'

Da-Wei laughed.

'Yes,' he replied. 'When we left Canton she was a little five-year-old girl. Now she is going back to Canton and she is a bank director!'

Da-Wei closed the book of newspaper articles and put it down. He looked at it thoughtfully.

'May has worked hard. She has been very successful. What will she do next?' he said.

10

'Every Dollar in the Bank is Safe'

June, 1940

May sat at her desk in the United States–Chinese Bank in Oakland. It was early, not yet eight o'clock, and the bank was quiet. It was a lovely spring day, and the morning sun shone through the large windows.

She read the international business news. There was a report in the newspaper about the branches of the United States–Chinese Bank in the Far East. The report said that the branches were doing very good business. May was thinking of opening one or two more branches – one in Singapore and another in Kuala Lumpur.

Someone knocked on the door.

'Come in!' May said.

She looked up as her secretary, Mei-Li, came into the office. Mei-Li was holding a cup of coffee and an envelope.

'Good morning, Miss Kan. This telegram[38] has just arrived from Hong Kong.'

Mei-Li walked over the thick carpets and stood in front of May's large desk.

'Thank you, Mei-Li.'

May took the telegram and smiled.

'Thanks for the coffee,' she said.

May opened the telegram. It was from the director of the United States–Chinese Bank in Hong Kong. The news was bad.

PEOPLE HERE IN HONG KONG WORRIED ABOUT THEIR MONEY. WE HAD TO PAY BACK HUNDREDS OF THOUSANDS OF DOLLARS TODAY. THE BANK RAN OUT OF MONEY. WE HAD TO CLOSE[39] THE BANK AT MIDDAY. SEND FIVE MILLION DOLLARS IMMEDIATELY.

May read the telegram again. It was impossible. The Hong Kong branch had run out of money! It had closed! There was no more money in the bank. It could not pay customers who asked for their money.

She looked at the telegram a third time. Why had this happened? Why had so many people suddenly taken their money out of the bank? There must be a reason.

May picked up the phone and began to dial a number, but there was another knock on the door.

'Come in!'

Mei-Li came into the room again. She looked worried.

'Miss Kan? There's a newspaper reporter in the office,' she said. 'He says that he has some questions about the Hong Kong branch. He says that the branch in Hong Kong is in trouble. He says that all our customers in Hong Kong asked for their money back and that the bank could not pay everybody. Do you want to talk with him?'

'No, I do not,' May answered.

'Well, what shall I tell him?'

May thought for a moment. She spoke quickly.

'Tell the reporter that there are no problems with the Hong Kong bank,' she said. 'He has heard stories about the bank but the stories are not true. The stories are coming from the Far East Bank. The Far East Bank is the other big bank in Hong Kong. The Far East Bank has not been doing good business. They want our customers. They want our customers to take their money to the Far East Bank.

'Tell the reporter that there is plenty of money in the United States–Chinese Bank in Hong Kong,' May went on. 'There is enough money to pay everybody. There is no reason to worry. Everybody will be paid.'

Mei-Li left the room and May read the telegram again. She knew that she had to do something quickly. She made a few notes on a piece of paper. Then she called for Mei-Li.

'I told the reporter what you said, Miss Kan,' Mei-Li said. 'But he laughed. He told me to read the newspapers tomorrow.'

'Don't worry about him, Mei-Li,' May replied. 'Now I have to contact the Canton and Shanghai branches of the bank. I want them to send some money to the Hong Kong branch immediately. A lot of money.'

'How much?' Mei-Li asked.

'Five million dollars,' May replied.

'But ... so much money? Does the Hong Kong branch need so much money?'

'Yes,' replied May quickly. 'And the branches of the bank in China have that much money and more. It will not be difficult for them to send the money to the Hong

Kong branch. The branches in China will get it back.'

There was silence for a few moments. Mei-Li did not move.

'Well, what is it?' May asked.

'I'm sorry, Miss Kan,' began Mei-Li, 'but —'

'But what, Mei-Li? What do you want to say? Hurry up, there isn't much time!'

'Please excuse me, Miss Kan, but my family – all our money is in the Hong Kong branch of the United States–Chinese Bank. My father and brothers have worked hard all their lives. When the bank opened a branch in Hong Kong, I told them to put their money into the bank. I said that their money would be safe. But now —'

Mei-Li looked down at the note she was holding.

'They're not going to lose all their money, are they, Miss Kan?' she continued. 'There will be enough money to pay everybody, won't there? The bank won't close, will it?'

'No, of course not!' said May. 'Of course there will be enough money to pay everybody. Nobody will lose anything. This is not a big problem. When the Hong Kong branch gets the money from China, it will be able to pay everybody. And when they see that, people will stop asking for their money.' Then she added, 'Don't worry, Mei-Li. Your family's money is quite safe. I promise you that. Every dollar in the Hong Kong branch is completely safe. All right?'

'Thank you, Miss Kan.' Mei-Li smiled.

'Now, get on with your work and don't worry,' May said.

'The bank won't close, will it?'

Mei-Li went to her office but came back immediately.

'Miss Kan, there's another telegram for you. It's just arrived. It's from Hong Kong.'

The secretary gave May the envelope and left the room, closing the door quietly behind her.

May put the telegram on her desk and looked at it for a few moments. She picked it up. Her hands were shaking. Then she opened the telegram and read it quickly. It was from the Hong Kong branch of the United States–Chinese Bank. The message was short.

CROWDS OUTSIDE THE BANK.

CANTON AND SHANGHAI BRANCHES NOW CLOSED.

May got up and went to the window. The United States–Chinese branches in Canton and Shanghai had also run out of money! May stood at the window. Although it was warm and sunny in the room, she felt cold. And for the second time in her life, she felt afraid.

11

'Our Customers Want Their Money Back'

Oakland, June 1940

May did not get home until midnight on that terrible day. Her mother and father met her at the front door. Yim-Ping looked quickly at May's pale, tired face and took her into the kitchen. She put a bowl of hot soup on the table and waited until May had finished eating it. Then Yim-Ping poured tea before she spoke.

'May, is it true what people are saying about the branches of the bank in China and Hong Kong? Is it true that there isn't any money in the branches? Is it true that people are going to lose all their money?'

'Yes, Mother, it's true. It's true,' May answered quietly.

'But how did it happen?' asked Da-Wei unhappily. 'How is it possible?'

'Well, a few months ago the branch in Hong Kong invested[40] a lot of money in a group of companies,' May replied. 'Some of those companies got into trouble[41]. A few of them closed down. The branch lost a lot of money that it had invested in the companies. But it still had enough money to do business. Then the trouble began. The only other big bank in Hong Kong is the Far East Bank. It's a smaller bank than our bank and they don't have so many customers.

'Anyway,' May went on. 'The Far East Bank heard

about the trouble. They heard about the money that our branch in Hong Kong had lost. The Far East Bank knew that our branch was weak. So they told everyone that our branch had no money. They told all the reporters at newspapers and radio stations. Our customers heard the stories and they were scared. They were frightened that they would lose their money. They went to the United States–Chinese Bank in Hong Kong to get their money.

'Hundreds of our customers went to the bank,' May continued. 'They all wanted their money back, at the same time. But the bank couldn't pay everybody back immediately. This all happened so quickly. Now all the United States–Chinese Banks in Asia are closed. I can't believe it. Yesterday, everything was fine.'

'But can't you do something?' asked Da-Wei. 'You must be able to do something!'

'Father, what can I do?' May replied. 'There is not enough money to pay all our customers. No bank can repay every customer at the same time. Tomorrow I'm going to fly to Hong Kong. But I don't know what I can do. Perhaps it's too late to do anything.'

Da-Wei drank a little tea. He looked old and tired.

'And if nothing can be done, will those people lose all their money?' Da-Wei asked. 'Will they lose everything? What about all our relatives in Canton? Will they be all right?'

May closed her eyes and put her hands on her face.

'Father, I'm sorry. I don't know. When people in China heard about the problems in Hong Kong, they wanted to get their money, too. Now the Canton and Shanghai branches of the United States–Chinese Bank have closed. All our customers in Hong Kong, Canton and Shanghai want their money back. And there isn't enough money to pay them all.' She got up and walked slowly across the room.

'I'm sorry, but I'm tired. I have to get up early tomorrow and take the plane to Hong Kong. Goodnight, Father. Goodnight, Mother.'

'May!' Yim-Ping's voice was angry. May looked at her in surprise.

'May! Come back here! Sit down! Why are you talking like this? You must do something! You must save those banks!'

'But I can't save them, Mother!' May replied. 'I've done everything that I can!'

She came back and sat down beside Yim-Ping.

'There's nothing more that I can do!' May said. 'There isn't enough money!'

Yim-Ping put her hand on May's shoulder.

'Listen, child,' she said gently. 'Thousands of people put their money in your banks. They trusted[42] you. They trusted you because they know your story. They knew that you began life in America with nothing. They knew that you couldn't speak English and you had no money. But you worked hard and you became successful. You became rich and powerful. People saw what you had done, and they knew that everything was possible. You gave hope to so many people.'

Yim-Ping put her hand on her daughter's arm.

'May, you mustn't take hope away from these people,'

she said. 'These people trusted you.'

May smiled at Yim-Ping.

'You're right, Mother. Don't worry,' she said. 'There is something that I can do. I will make sure that all the bank's customers get their money back.'

Then she picked up her briefcase and went into her room.

And all that night, whenever Yim-Ping went and stood outside her daughter's door, she saw that the light was on and she could hear her daughter talking quietly on the telephone.

A few days later, there was another newspaper article for Yim-Ping to put into her book.

June, 1940

THE HONG KONG BRANCH OF THE UNITED STATES–CHINESE BANK OPENS FOR BUSINESS AGAIN

THE Hong Kong branch of the United States–Chinese Bank will open for business again today.

Miss May Kan, the director of the United States–Chinese Bank in Oakland, California, flew to Hong Kong yesterday. Soon after she arrived in Hong Kong today she spoke to newspaper reporters and to a crowd of the bank's customers:

'Ladies and Gentlemen. The Hong Kong branch of the United States–Chinese Bank will open again tomorrow. Customers may take their money out of the bank at any time. The bank will stay open all night. The staff of the bank will work all night so that customers who want to take out their money can be paid immediately. And *everyone* will be paid.

'However, I say to our customers, "Your money is safe. You do not need to take your money out of the bank."

'The bank would also like to thank its customers for their trust at this time. All customers who leave their money in the bank will receive a 10% bonus[43] at the end of the year. We are sorry for the trouble and we are happy to offer our customers this special bonus. Thank you for your trust in the United States–Chinese Bank.'

A crowd was waiting outside the bank in Hong Kong. The people had read the article in the newspaper. They had read May's words. Their voices were silent now but nobody left the crowd and went back to work.

'Get in line!' someone shouted.

People began to stand in line. Soon hundreds of people were standing in line. Then the doors of the bank opened. The people at the front of the line went into the bank. They stopped in surprise. Beside each cashier[44] there were tall piles of banknotes. The first customers in the line stared at the banknotes.

'There must be millions of dollars here!' someone said.

'Yes, sir, there are,' replied a cashier, smiling. 'And how

may I help you, sir? Would you like more information about the end-of-year bonus?'

The first customers looked at the piles of banknotes. They looked back at the smiling cashiers.

'Well, yes,' one of the customers said. 'Yes. Tell me about it.'

People in the line began to move forward. All the bank's customers who wanted to take out their money were paid immediately. Many other customers saw the piles of money and they decided to leave their money in the bank. At 6.30 p.m. that evening, the last customer went into the bank. There were still piles of banknotes beside the cashiers.

12

'$5 000 000 Are Missing'

Oakland, 1940

May was away from America for three weeks. From Hong Kong, she travelled to Canton. After a few days there, she took a plane to Shanghai. She worked hard. She spoke to the staff in the branches of the banks and thanked them for their hard work. She talked to newspaper reporters and to radio reporters. She explained why the banks had closed. She explained that the banks had paid every customer who wanted their money.

And after two weeks, all the branches of the United States–Chinese Bank were working normally again. May was now famous. The Chinese newspapers printed articles about her. They called her, 'The Woman of Iron'. She received hundreds of telegrams from America, Hong Kong and all over China. 'Well done and thank you,' the telegrams said. She was invited to dinners, parties and lunches. She went to them all.

In America, there was a report on the television about May and the bank's troubles in Hong Kong and China. Yim-Ping and Da-Wei watched their daughter on the television. Yim-Ping saw how thin and tired May was. Yim-Ping shook her head unhappily.

'There's something wrong, husband,' she said to Da-Wei. 'May looks ill. She looks terrible. Why isn't she pleased? The papers say that she saved those branches. They call her "The Woman of Iron"! But look at her!

What is the matter with her?'

Da-Wei switched off the television.

'Don't worry about May,' he replied. 'The papers are right – she was always as strong as iron. Do you remember when she was a child and she unbound her feet? She didn't care that you were angry with her! And remember how she got up at five o'clock every morning and taught herself to read English! She'll be OK. I think that she's very tired. She's been travelling a lot and working too hard.'

Yim-Ping shook her head. She knew there was something wrong with her daughter.

'Well, I hope that she comes home soon,' she said. 'I hope that she's not ill.'

Business in the Hong Kong, Shanghai and Canton branches returned to normal[45] after two weeks. And after three weeks, business was better than ever before. It was time for May to return to America. When she arrived in California, she went to her office. Mei-Li jumped up from her desk when she saw May.

'Miss Kan! You're back!'

May sat at her desk and closed her eyes.

Mei-Li looked closely at her.

'Miss Kan? Are you all right? Why don't you go home and rest today? You must be tired after your long journey.'

May opened her eyes and smiled.

'Thanks, Mei-Li, but I'm all right,' she said. 'I don't want to go home. I want to be in the office. Don't worry. I'll be OK. Could you get me some coffee, please?'

'Yes, of course.'

May waited until Mei-Li was out of the room, then she got up slowly, crossed the room and opened a bookcase. There was a knock on the door.

'Yes?'

'There are two men here, Miss Kan,' said Mei-Li. 'They're FBI[46] agents. They'd like to speak to you. What shall I tell them?'

'Tell them to come in.'

Mei-Li brought the two men into May's office. One of the men was Chinese. He took a badge from one of his coat pockets.

'Good morning, Miss Kan,' he said as he showed her the badge. 'We're from the FBI. My name's Tan.'

'How do you do, gentlemen,' May replied. 'Please sit down.'

The men looked at each other. They did not sit down. There was a moment's silence.

May sat at her desk and looked up at the two men.

'What can I do for you, gentlemen?' she asked.

'Miss Kan, there are some questions that we have to ask you,' said Tan.

'And what are your questions about, gentlemen?'

'Well,' said Tan. 'Five million dollars are missing from the United States–Chinese Bank here in Oakland.'

'Oh.'

'The money disappeared when you left America to go to Hong Kong.'

'Did it?' May stared out of the window.

'Do you know anything about this money, Miss Kan?' asked Tan.

'We're from the FBI. My name's Tan.'

May looked back at the FBI agents and smiled.

'Gentlemen,' she said,' I know about that money. I took it. I needed it. I couldn't let the branches in Hong Kong and China close. Too many people would have lost everything. I had to do it. I knew what I was doing.'

'A lot of my relatives are in Hong Kong,' said Tan. 'You did the right thing.'

'Yes, I did the right thing,' said May, 'but I'm not sure that the directors of the United States–Chinese Bank will agree with me. Bank directors do not like people taking large sums of money from their bank without asking.'

May began to put away the papers on her desk. 'I guess that this is the end of my time as a banker, gentlemen,' she said. 'What happens now?'

The two men looked quickly at each other.

'We must ask you to come with us to the FBI office here in Oakland,' Tan replied.

May stood up.

'Certainly, gentlemen,' she replied. 'But there's something that I'd like to do before we go.'

May went to the bookcase and took down a large, heavy book and a small wooden box. She took some coins from the box and threw them onto her desk six times. Then she began to turn the pages of the book. She began to read:

'Do not worry about what happened in the past.
If you lose your horse, do not run after it;
It will come back to you.
You will be lucky.'

May shut the book and looked at the two men. She smiled.

'Now,' she said, 'I'm ready. Shall we go?'

POINTS FOR UNDERSTANDING

Points for Understanding

1

1 What happened to the daughters of rich families?
2 Why did Mei-Ying not want to have her feet bound?
3 Where did Mei-Ying go when she ran out of the house?
4 What did Mei-Ying ask the little girl?

2

1 Why did the man have a wooden collar round his neck?
2 Where did Mei-Ying find her father?
3 What was one of the important things that Mei-Ying's father said to her grandfather?

3

1 Why did Mei-Ying's mother not want to go to America?
2 What did Mei-Ying's grandfather not want to leave in China?
3 What did Qin Jin, the Chinese poet, do that Mei-Ying also did?
4 Why do you think that Mei-Ying wanted to go to America?

4

1 Why did Mei-Ying want her mother to call her May?
2 Why was Powell Street important to Mei-Ying?
3 Where did Da-Wei keep his money?

5

1 What did May read to help her to learn English?
2 How did May and her father get Yim-Ping out of the building?
3 Why did May's father want to get to his shop quickly?
4 Where did the Kan family go after the San Francisco earthquake?

6

1 What was one of the things that May did on Chinese New Year's Day?
2 Why did May want to work in her father's shop? Give two reasons.
3 What did Yim-Ping say?

7

1 Why did Da-Wei keep his money in shoe boxes?
2 What did Da-Wei and May do one day?
3 What was May's idea?

8

1 Where did May have to go to see her Chinese customers?
2 What did Yim-Ping say to May about her new job?

9

1 What happened to May six years after she began to work in the bank?
2 Why was the United States–Chinese Bank better for Chinese people than other American banks?
3 The reporter asked May, 'Are you Chinese or American?' What was the answer?

10

1 What happened to the Hong Kong branch of the bank?
2 What was May's promise to Mei-Li?
3 Why did May feel afraid for the second time in her life?

11

1 What did the Far East Bank tell the news reporters?
2 Write two things that May said to the reporters when she arrived in Hong Kong.
3 What did the bank's customers see when the bank opened its doors again?

12

1 What did the Chinese newspapers call May?
2 Write two things that May did when she was in China and in Hong Kong.
3 What did the men from the FBI say to May?
4 What had May done? Why?

GLOSSARY

Glossary

1 ***bound*** – *to bind, to have one's feet bound* (page 4)
to have a long piece of cloth tied tightly round the feet to keep them small. Many years ago, the daughters of rich men in China had their feet bound when they were very young. When they were adults, these rich women could not walk easily. This was a sign that their family was rich and that they had servants. Servants and poor people in China did not have their feet bound and their feet were 'big, ugly feet'.

2 ***combs*** (page 8)
pieces of flat plastic, wood or metal with small thin 'teeth'. You comb your hair to tidy it.

3 ***paused*** – *to pause* (page 8)
to stop speaking for a short time.

4 ***courtyard*** (page 10)
an open area in the middle of a house with rooms around all four sides.

5 ***silk*** (page 11)
soft, shiny material that was used to make clothes for rich people.

6 ***temples*** (page 11)
places where people go to pray.

7 ***dragon*** (page 14)
a very large magical animal. Dragons have big eyes, sharp teeth and long tails (See the illustration on page 15). They can blow fire from their mouths.

8 ***wooden collar*** (page 14)
a heavy piece of wood that was put round the neck of a criminal. The collar was so big that the criminal could not touch his own mouth with his hands.

9 ***whispered*** – *to whisper* (page 16)
to speak very quietly.

10 ***shrine*** (page 16)
a place in their houses or shops where people prayed to the gods. Many houses in China had special gods for their family. The family prayed to the *family gods* at the *family shrine*. They asked for good luck or money.

11 ***incense*** (page 16)
incense is made from the seeds, stems and the dried juice of special plants. It has a strong smell when it burns. Incense is often made into long, thin sticks and burnt in temples to show respect to the gods.

12 ***'Little Flower'*** (page 18)
a nice name to call a girl child.

13 ***members of the family*** (page 23)
your aunts and uncles and their children, your grandfathers and grandmothers. These people are your *relatives*.

14 ***carved coffin*** (page 23)
people who die are put into a wooden box, called a coffin. This box can have flowers or pictures carved in the wood.

15 ***I Ching*** (page 24)
a Chinese book written thousands of years ago. It contains advice on how to live.

16 ***Chinatown*** (page 26)
a part of a city in a country outside China where only Chinese people live. There are Chinatowns in London, New York and some other big cities.

17 ***with difficulty*** (page 26)
Mei-Ying could not walk easily. Her feet were very painful.

18 ***making a lot of money*** – *to make a lot money* (page 32)
the business was very successful. You can *make a lot of money* by working very hard.

19 ***crash*** (page 35)
when something heavy falls to the ground, it makes a loud noise – *crash*! When a car hits another car, they crash.

20 ***Chinese New Year*** (page 39)
the first day of New Year for Chinese people. The months of the Chinese year follow the thirty days from a new moon to the full moon. So the first day of the Chinese New Year is on a different day of the Christian calendar each year.

21 ***jazz, baseball, apple pie*** (page 39)
examples of American music, sport and food.

22 ***traditional Chinese celebrations*** (page 39)
Chinese New Year is a time for traditional celebrations. Special food is eaten and houses are cleaned. A lot of decorations are put up. The colour red is used for decoration. Red is the colour of good luck for Chinese people.

23 ***Chinese characters*** (page 39)
the Chinese language is written with characters, not letters.
24 ***oysters and seaweed*** (page 40)
oysters are seafood. Seaweed is like grass. It is a vegetable that grows in the sea. The Chinese words for 'oysters' and 'seaweed' sound the same as the Chinese words for 'good business' and 'prosperity'. (See Glossary No. 25)
25 ***'good business'* and *'prosperity'*** (page 40)
a way of saying to someone, 'You will have good luck and success in business.'
26 ***chopsticks*** (page 42)
two long, thin pieces of wood used to carry food to the mouth.
27 ***do business*** (page 42)
to buy or sell something in a shop or to have customers (e.g. a bank).
28 ***profit*** (page 46)
the money that you have left after you have paid all your costs.
29 ***main branch*** (of a bank) (page 48)
large banks often have smaller offices, or branches, in different cities or countries. A *main branch* is a large, important office of the bank.
30 ***the American way of banking*** (page 50)
the way of banking in the United States.
31 ***do your paperwork*** (page 52)
the written work that is part of office work.
32 ***director*** (of the bank) (page 56)
a person who has a very important position in a company, a bank, etc.
33 ***proud*** – *to be proud* (page 56)
to be very pleased and happy about something or someone.
34 ***lion dances*** (page 57)
traditional Chinese dances. A long line of dancers wear a costume that covers their heads and bodies. The costume looks like a lion's head and body.
35 ***borrow*** – *to borrow* (page 57)
to be given money by the bank. The money will have to be repaid after a certain time.
36 ***lend*** – *to lend* (page 57)
to give customers of the bank some money. This money has to be repaid after a certain time.

37 ***Dior suit*** (page 61)
expensive and fashionable clothes for women that are made by a famous company in France.

38 ***telegram*** (page 65)
at the time of this story, people could not easily make international phone calls. The fastest way to send important information was by telegraph. Telegraph machines sent messages along electric wires. The words of the message were then written down. This piece of paper was called a telegram. Letters took many days to arrive. Telegrams arrived in a few hours.

39 ***close*** – *to close* (page 66)
to close the doors of a bank for a period of time. The customers cannot come in and take the money out.

40 ***invested in*** – *to invest in* (page 71)
to put your money into a bank or a company in order to get more money back after a period of time.

41 ***got into trouble*** – *to get into trouble* (page 71)
to have problems and maybe lose money or close down.

42 ***trusted*** – *to trust, to put your trust in* (page 73)
to believe that someone will always do the right thing for you.

43 ***bonus*** (page 75)
extra money that you receive as well as the money you usually get.

44 ***cashier*** (page 76)
a man or woman in a bank who pays money to customers.

45 ***returned to normal*** – *to return to normal* (page 79)
the banks are now doing their usual business.

46 ***FBI*** (page 80)
the Federal Bureau of Investigation, the criminal investigation department in the United States of America.

INTERMEDIATE LEVEL

Oliver Twist *by Charles Dickens*
The Bonetti Inheritance *by Richard Prescott*
No Comebacks *by Frederick Forsyth*
The Enchanted April *by Elizabeth von Arnim*
The Three Strangers *by Thomas Hardy*
The Smuggler *by Piers Plowright*
The Pearl *by John Steinbeck*
The Woman Who Disappeared *by Philip Prowse*
A Town Like Alice *by Nevil Shute*
The Queen of Death *by John Milne*
Meet Me in Istanbul *by Richard Chisholm*
The Great Gatsby *by F. Scott Fitzgerald*
The Space Invaders *by Geoffrey Matthews*
My Cousin Rachel *by Daphne du Maurier*
I'm the King of the Castle *by Susan Hill*
Dracula *by Bram Stoker*
The Speckled Band and Other Stories *by Sir Arthur Conan Doyle*
The Queen of Spades and Other Stories *by Aleksandr Pushkin*
The Diamond Hunters *by Wilbur Smith*
When Rain Clouds Gather *by Bessie Head*
Banker *by Dick Francis*
No Longer at Ease *by Chinua Achebe*
The Franchise Affair *by Josephine Tey*
The Case of the Lonely Lady *by John Milne*
Silas Marner *by George Eliot*
Pride and Prejudice *by Jane Austen*
Wuthering Heights *by Emily Bronte*
Jurassic Park *by Michael Crichton*

For further information on the full selection of Readers at all five levels in the series, please refer to the Heinemann ELT Readers catalogue.

Macmillan Heinemann English Language Teaching

A division of Macmillan Publishers Limited

Companies and representatives throughout the world

ISBN 0 435 27300 0

First published 1999

Editorial development by Phoenix Publishing Services
Illustrated by Kay Dixey
Typography by Adrian Hodgkins
Designed by Sue Vaudin
Cover by Kim McGillivray and Marketplace Design
Typeset in 11/14.5pt Goudy
Printed and bound in Spain by Mateu Cromo

99 00 01 02 10 9 8 7 6 5 4 3 2 1